ARCHAEOPTERYX

AND OTHER FLYING DINOSAURS

Prehistoric World

ARCHAEOPTERYX

AND OTHER FLYING DINOSAURS

VIRGINIA SCHOMP

BENCHMARK BOOKS

MARSHALL CAVENDISH
NEW YORK

DINOSAURS LIVED MILLIONS OF YEARS AGO. EVERYTHING WE KNOW ABOUT THEM—HOW THEY LOOKED, WALKED, ATE, FOUGHT, MATED, AND RAISED THEIR YOUNG—COMES FROM EDUCATED GUESSES BY THE SCIENTISTS WHO DISCOVER AND STUDY FOSSILS. THE INFORMATION IN THIS BOOK IS BASED ON WHAT MOST SCIENTISTS BELIEVE RIGHT NOW. TOMORROW OR NEXT WEEK OR NEXT YEAR, NEW DISCOVERIES COULD LEAD TO NEW IDEAS. SO KEEP YOUR EYES AND EARS OPEN FOR NEWS FLASHES FROM THE PREHISTORIC WORLD!

Benchmark Books
Marshall Cavendish
99 White Plains Road
Tarrytown, New York 10591-9001
www.marshallcavendish.com

© Marshall Cavendish Corporation 2004

Library of Congress Cataloging-in-Publication Data

Schomp, Virginia.
  Archaeopteryx and other flying dinosaurs/ Virginia Schomp.
      v. cm. — (Prehistoric world)
Includes bibliographical references and index.
Contents: The puzzling "dinosaur birds" — Time line: the age of dinosaurs — Jurassic islands — Map: the late Jurassic world — Up in the air — Dinosaurs all around us.
  ISBN 0-7614-1546-7
  1. Archaeopteryx — Juvenile literature. 2. Birds, Fossil — Juvenile literature.
[1. Archaeopteryx. 2. Birds, Fossil. 3. Dinosaurs.] I. Title. II. Series: Schomp, Virginia. Prehistoric world.

Front cover: *Archaeopteryx*   Back cover: *Iberomesornis*   Page 2: *Gobipteryx*

Photo Credits:

Cover illustration: The Natural History Museum, London / John Sibbick

The illustrations and photographs in this book are used by permission and through the courtesy of: *Marshall Cavendish Corporation:* 2, 11, 12-13, 14, 15, 18, 20-21, 22, 23, back cover. *The Natural History Museum, London:* 24; De Agostini, 8-9; John Sibbick, 17.

Map and Dinosaur Family Tree by Robert Romagnoli

Printed in China

1 3 5 6 4 2

For Kailene Nye

Contents

THE PUZZLING "DINOSAUR-BIRDS"

A steamy forest in central Europe, 150 million years ago. A herd of long-necked dinosaurs rest in the shade of the evergreens. Lizards and small furry mammals rustle underfoot. An insect buzzes through the warm air.

Suddenly there is a squawk and a flash of color. A small feathered creature swoops down and sinks its teeth into the insect. Using its clawed feet, the creature lands on a tree branch. Then, with a gulp, the *Archaeopteryx* swallows its snack.

Birdlike Archaeopteryx *lived on a diet of insects, worms, and other small creatures.*

Dinosaurs ruled the earth for 165 million years. Around the middle of that long time period, creatures with wings and feathers began to appear. Some looked a lot like modern birds. Others had unbirdlike features that would look strange to us today. The first and most famous of these puzzling creatures was *Archaeopteryx*.

The Age of Dinosaurs

Dinosaurs walked the earth during the Mesozoic era, also known as the Age of Dinosaurs. The Mesozoic era lasted from about 250 million to 65 million years ago. It is divided into three periods: the Triassic, Jurassic, and Cretaceous.

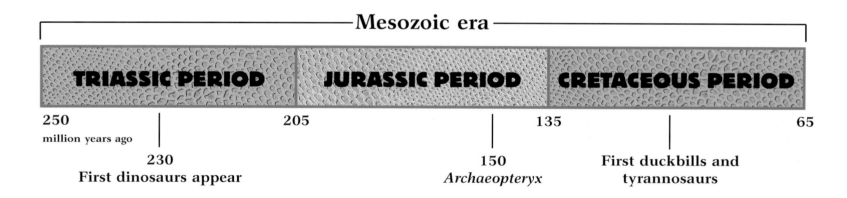

MONONYKUS
(mon-uh-NIKE-us)
When: Late Cretaceous,
85–70 million years ago
Where: Mongolia
- Short arms ended in
  single claws
- Ran fast on long legs

Flightless Mononykus *had birdlike bones and feathers but it also had unbirdlike arms, a long tail, and sharp teeth.*

HALF BIRD, HALF DINOSAUR

Paleontologists (scientists who study prehistoric life) dug up the first *Archaeopteryx* skeleton in 1861. They were excited—and confused. The fossil looked like a dinosaur. It had sharp teeth, clawed fingers, scaly legs, and a long bony tail. But it also looked like a bird. Its bird-like features included a wishbone, clawed feet, wings, and feathers. The feathers were shaped exactly like those on a modern flying bird.

Some paleontologists decided that *Archaeopteryx* was an early bird—maybe the first bird ever. Others thought that it was a special kind of winged, feathered, meat-eating dinosaur. Today scientists are still arguing the question. And they continue to study ancient fossils to learn more about *Archaeopteryx* and its world.

Archaeopteryx *means "ancient wing." Scientists still cannot agree on whether this puzzling winged creature was a birdlike dinosaur or a dinosaur-like bird.*

ARCHAEOPTERYX
(ar-kee-OP-ter-icks)
When: Late Jurassic,
   150 million years ago
Where: Germany
◆ About 14 inches long; weighed
   about 2 pounds—about the size
   of a large parrot
◆ Three clawed fingers on each wing

IBEROMESORNIS
(eye-ber-oh-mess-OR-nis)
When: Early Cretaceous,
130–120 million years ago
Where: Spain
• Tail shorter than a dinosaur's
 but longer than a modern bird's
• About the size of a sparrow

Like Archaeopteryx, Iberomesornis *had wings, feathers, and short pointy teeth in its long narrow jaws.*

14

Is There a Dinosaur in Your House?

Was *Archaeopteryx* the great-great-great-granddaddy of your pet canary? Some paleontologists say yes. They believe that this puzzling "dinosaur-bird" belonged to a group of animals called avialans. On page 26, you can see how these scientists fit *Archaeopteryx* and its closest cousins into the dinosaur family tree.

Early avialans had wings and feathers plus sharp teeth and long tails. Later avialans had shorter tails and toothless beaks. We call these later avialans birds. So *Archaeopteryx* and your pet songbird could be very close relatives.

Other scientists say that modern birds did not descend from *Archaeopteryx*. Instead, *Archaeopteryx* and the birds developed separately from the same long-ago ancestor. That ancestor was probably a small theropod (two-legged meat-eating dinosaur) that looked a lot like later theropods such as *Velociraptor* or *Deinonychus*. If that idea is right, *Archaeopteryx* and your canary are distant relatives, and today's birds are living, breathing dinosaurs.

Deinonychus *was a small theropod that lived toward the end of the Age of Dinosaurs. Many scientists believe that birds descended from one of the earliest theropods.*

JURASSIC ISLANDS

The middle part of the Age of Dinosaurs is called the Jurassic period. This was a time of endless summer, when the world was warm and wet year-round.

At the beginning of the Jurassic period, all the lands on earth were joined in one huge continent surrounded by sea. In time that super-continent broke up. The two landmasses, Laurasia and Gondwanaland, drifted apart. Seawater flooded once-dry lands, and sea breezes carried rain to the deserts. The world grew a thick green carpet of ferns, cycads, low bushes, and tall evergreens.

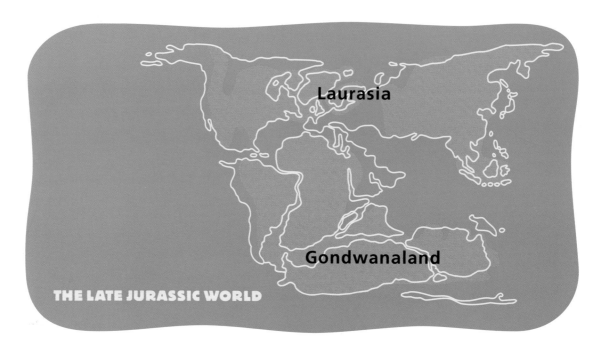

The green shading on the map shows the world's landmasses in Late Jurassic times. Over the centuries, the two large continents would split up and drift apart to form the modern continents, outlined in yellow.

Lush green plants surround a Jurassic swamp. The small trees are cycads, a kind of plant with palmlike leaves that was a favorite food of many plant-eating dinosaurs.

ALONG ANCIENT SHORES

Let's take a trip back in time 150 million years. We are visiting the part of Europe that will one day be called Germany. In Late Jurassic times, much of Europe is covered by shallow saltwater lagoons. Small islands dot the water. *Archaeopteryx* lives on these islands. We may find it perched in the treetops or patrolling the shoreline, searching for food.

We might also see other ancient animals. A small theropod runs along the shore, trying to catch a tiny lizard for lunch. In the water, there are fish, crocodiles, and fast-swimming ichthyosaurs—reptiles that look a lot like dolphins. Overhead, giant pterosaurs soar. The wings on these flying reptiles are made of skin, not feathers. Some pterosaurs have wings as wide as a fighter jet.

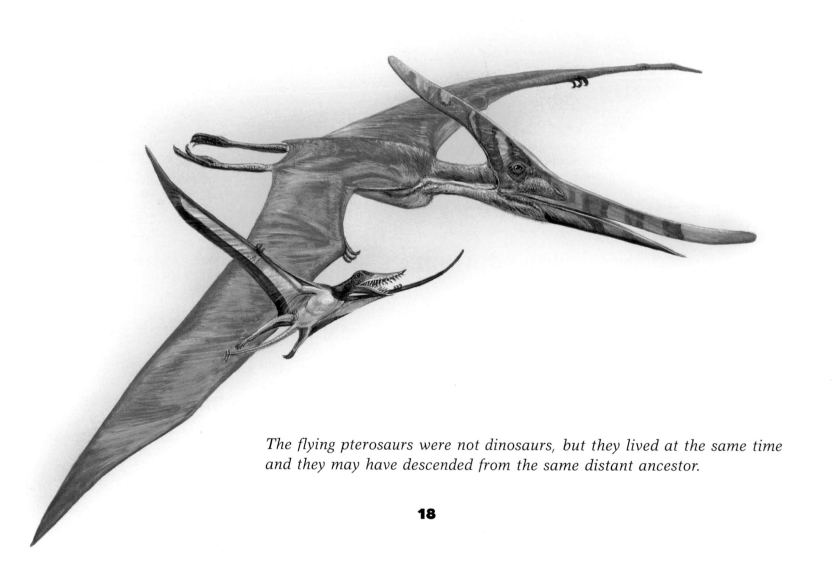

The flying pterosaurs were not dinosaurs, but they lived at the same time and they may have descended from the same distant ancestor.

UP IN THE AIR

*A*rchaeopteryx probably could fly, but not very far and not very well. It did not have the special breastbone and strong muscles that modern birds use for flying. This dinosaur-bird may have spent most of its time on the ground. Walking along the shore, it gobbled up worms, small lizards, and stranded fish and crabs. To catch a juicy moth or fly, it might run fast and use its wings to make short, clumsy, fluttering flights. Sometimes it might wade into the shallow water to do a little fishing.

Some paleontologists believe that *Archaeopteryx* lived not on the ground but mainly in small trees. It could have used its sharp clawed fingers to climb up the tree trunks. Then it would launch itself. Spreading its wings, *Archaeopteryx* would glide through the air to another tree or to the ground.

Toothy Hesperornis *could not fly at all. It spent most of its time floating and fishing in the warm waters that covered much of North America in the Late Cretaceous period.*

HESPERORNIS
(hess-per-OR-niss)
When: Late Cretaceous,
88–75 million years ago
Where: North America
* Long neck and long
  pointed beak
* Strong back legs and
  webbed feet for swimming

21

Archaeopteryx's small pointy teeth were good for gripping fish and other slippery meals. They were not much good for chewing, though. The winged hunter probably swallowed most of its meals whole.

Those small teeth were not made for self-defense either. If a hungry crocodile or theropod threatened, *Archaeopteryx* probably did not stop to fight. Instead, it ran as fast as it could. Flapping its wings, it tried to leap and flutter its way to safety.

ICHTHYORNIS
(ick-thee-OR-niss)
When: Late Cretaceous, 70 million years ago
Where: Kansas
◆ Large breastbone and wishbone for flying
◆ Short bony tail

An Ichthyornis *uses its sharp teeth to eat an ammonoid, a kind of shellfish that lived throughout the Age of Dinosaurs.*

GOBIPTERYX
(go-BIP-ter-icks)
When: Late Cretaceous,
  80–75 million years ago
Where: Mongolia
◆ Long wings and strong
  muscles for flying
◆ Toothless beak

Gobipteryx *was a large flying dinosaur or early bird that measured up to five feet long and weighed about as much as a German shepherd.*

EGGS AND BABIES

We do not know how *Archaeopteryx* cared for its young. Like all dinosaurs, the babies most likely hatched from eggs. Paleontologists have found fossil eggs of one of *Archaeopteryx*'s close relatives, *Gobipteryx*. Inside the eggshells were babies that had been nearly ready to hatch. The babies' wing bones were almost fully grown. That might mean that *Gobipteryx* was able to fly soon after hatching.

Could newly hatched *Archaeopteryx* leave the nest, too? Or did parents take care of their babies the way modern birds do? Someday scientists may find fossils from an *Archaeopteryx* nest to help them answer these questions.

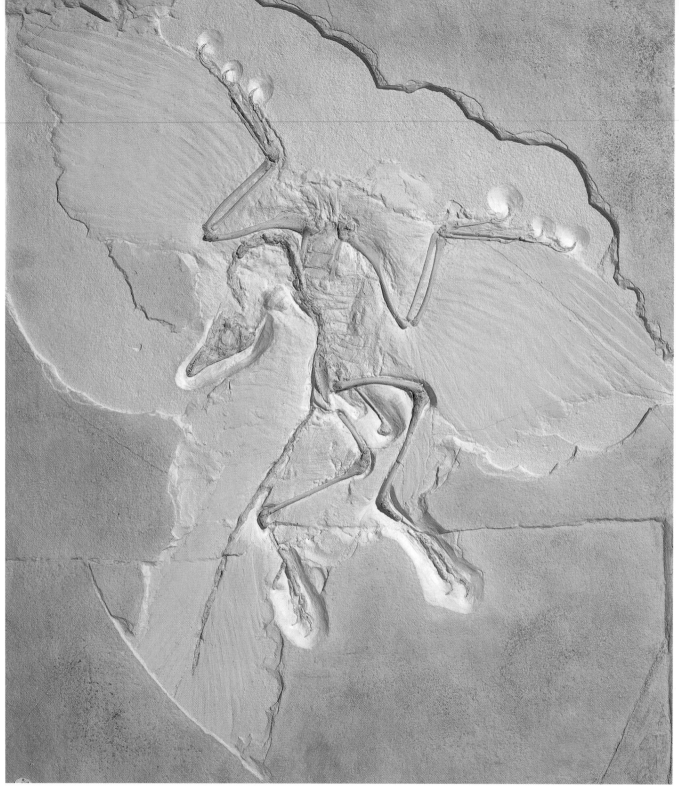

This amazingly detailed fossil was found in a limestone quarry in southern Germany. Preserved in the fine-grained rock are an Archaeopteryx's bones and traces of its wings and feathers.

DINOSAURS ALL AROUND US

The last *Archaeopteryx* lived 150 million years ago. Other kinds of dinosaur-birds survived right up to the end of the Age of Dinosaurs, alongside the first true birds. Then, around 65 million years ago, the remaining dinosaurs died out. No one knows why *Archaeopteryx* became extinct when it did or what killed all the dinosaurs.

Some animals survived the great dinosaur disappearance—snakes, turtles, insects, fish, crocodiles, and mammals. The birds survived, too. In fact, today there are more than ten thousand different kinds of birds. If birds really did descend from dinosaurs, that means a bit of the prehistoric world lives on with us today.

Dinosaur Family Tree

ORDER
All dinosaurs are divided into two large groups, based on the shape and position of their hipbones. Saurischians had forward-pointing hipbones.

SUBORDER
Theropods were two-legged meat-eating dinosaurs.

INFRAORDER
Tetanurans had stiffened (not flexible) tails.

FAMILY
A family includes one or more types of closely related dinosaurs.

GENUS
Every dinosaur has a two-word name. The first word tells us what genus, or type, of dinosaur it is. The genus plus the second word are its species—the group of very similar animals it belongs to. (For example, *Archaeopteryx lithographica* is one species of *Archaeopteryx*.)

Scientists organize all living things into groups, according to features shared. This chart shows one possible grouping of the "dinosaur-birds" in this book.

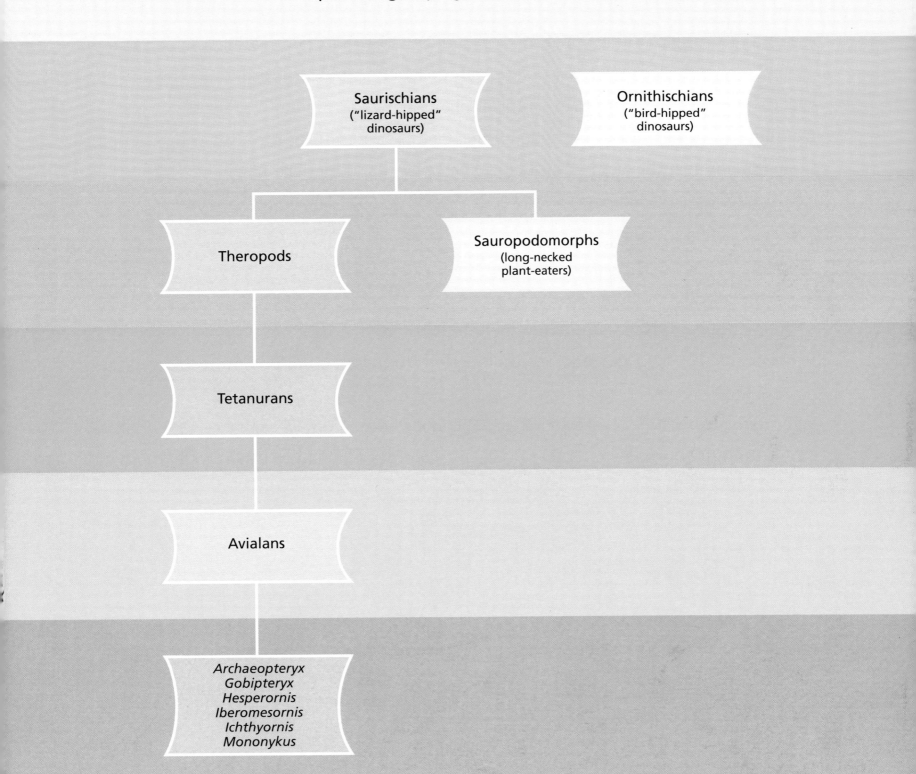

Glossary

avialans (ay-vee-YAY-lans): a group of animals with wings and feathers, which may have included dinosaurs such as *Archaeopteryx* as well as modern birds

cycads (SIE-kuds): low-growing tropical plants with sharp palmlike leaves

Deinonychus (die-NO-ni-kus): a small meat-eating dinosaur of the Cretaceous period that had many features similar to both *Archaeopteryx* and modern birds

extinct: no longer existing; an animal is extinct when every one of its kind has died

fossils: the hardened remains or traces of animals or plants that lived many thousands or millions of years ago

ichthyosaurs (ICK-thee-oh-sores): swimming reptiles that measured up to forty-five feet long and lived from 245 million to 90 million years ago

Jurassic (joo-RA-sick) **period:** the time period from about 205 million to 135 million years ago, when *Archaeopteryx* lived

lagoons: shallow bodies of water that are connected to a larger sea

paleontologists (pay-lee-on-TAH-luh-jists): scientists who study fossils to learn about dinosaurs and other forms of prehistoric life

pterosaurs (TEHR-uh-sores): flying reptiles with wings up to nearly forty feet across, which lived throughout most of the Age of Dinosaurs

theropods: a group of two-legged meat-eating dinosaurs with sharp teeth, clawed back feet, and short arms

wishbone: a V-shaped bone in the upper chest of *Archaeopteryx*, modern birds, and some small theropods

Find Out More

Books

Gaines, Richard M. *Archaeopteryx.* Edina, MN: ABDO Publishing, 2001.

The Humongous Book of Dinosaurs. New York: Stewart, Tabori, and Chang, 1997.

Marshall, Chris, ed. *Dinosaurs of the World.* 11 vols. New York: Marshall Cavendish, 1999.

Parker, Steve. *The Age of the Dinosaurs.* Vol. 5, *Dinosaurs and Birds.* Danbury, CT: Grolier Educational, 2000.

Sandell, Elizabeth J. *Archaeopteryx.* Naples, FL: Bancroft-Sage, 1989.

Schlein, Miriam. *The Puzzle of the Dinosaur-Bird.* New York: Dial Books for Young Readers, 1996.

Steele, Philip. *Extinct Birds and Those in Danger of Extinction.* New York: Franklin Watts, 1991.

ON-LINE SOURCES *

***Canadian Museum of Nature Online* at http://www.nature.ca/notebooks/english/mon2.htm**
The Canadian Museum of Nature's *Natural History Notebooks* provide lots of interesting facts and illustrations relating to 246 animal species, past and present. Click on "Prehistoric Life" for animals including *Archaeopteryx* as well as dinosaur-related topics such as Dinosaur Eggs and Dinosaur Extinction.

***Disappearance* at http://library.thinkquest.org/26615/index.htm**
Students in Singapore created this colorful website for the 1999 ThinkQuest Internet Challenge competition. The site focuses on endangered and extinct species and offers extensive information on seventy-six dinosaurs, including *Archaeopteryx*.

***Famous Feathered Fossils: Archaeopteryx Exhibit, Morrison Natural History Museum* at http://town.morrison.co.us/mnhm/Exhibits/Archae.html**
Visit this website of the Morrison Natural History Museum in Colorado to see photos of the museum's *Archaeopteryx* exhibit, which includes casts of seven *Archaeopteryx* fossils.

***Zoom Dinosaurs* at http://www.zoomdinosaurs.com**
This colorful site from Enchanted Learning Software includes a world of information on dinosaur-related topics: dinosaur myths, records, behavior, and fossils; dinosaur fact sheets; quizzes, puzzles, printouts, and crafts; tips on writing a school report; and more. Click on "Dinosaurs and Birds" for a look at *Archaeopteryx* and other birdlike dinosaurs.

*Website addresses sometimes change. For more on-line sources, check with the media specialist at your local library.

Index

Virginia Schomp grew up in a quiet suburban town in northeastern New Jersey, where eight-ton duck-billed dinosaurs once roamed. In first grade she discovered that she loved books and writing, and in sixth grade she was named "class bookworm," because she always had her nose in a book. Today she is a freelance author who has written more than forty books for young readers on topics including careers, animals, ancient cultures, and modern history. Ms. Schomp lives in the Catskill Mountain region of New York with her husband, Richard, and their son, Chip.